Tre

of the Noiiiwesi

Alaska, Western Canada & the Northwestern United States

Subalpine larch.

J. Duane Sept

Calypso Publishing

Calypso Publishing   www.calypso-publishing.com
P. O. Box 1141
Sechelt, BC, Canada
V0N 3A0
Duane Sept Photography   www.septphoto.com

Library and Archives Canada Cataloguing in Publication

Sept, J. Duane, 1950-
      Trees of the Northwest : Alaska, western Canada & the northwestern United States / J. Duane Sept.

Includes bibliographical references and index.
ISBN 978-0-9739819-4-0

      1. Trees--Northwest Coast of North America--Identification. 2. Trees--British Columbia--Pacific Coast--Identification. 3. Trees--Ecology. 4. Indians of North America--Northwest Coast of North America. 5. Traditional ecological knowledge--Northwest Coast of North America. I. Title.

QK477.2.I4S47 2011   582.16'09795   C2011-901044-5

Contents

Introduction

In the Pacific Northwest, native trees make up an essential part of most ecosystems from Alaska to northern California. These diverse species provide food and shelter for thousands of plants and animals living here. This guide identifies and describes the species of trees present in the region, including taller shrubs (maximum height of at least 33' (10 m).

Trees can be classified into two general groups: coniferous and deciduous. Coniferous trees keep their narrow leaves (needles) during the winter. These needles are coated with wax to prevent water loss, and are filled with resin to help them withstand freezing temperatures.

Deciduous trees normally lose their leaves in the fall and remain dormant in the winter so that they can survive until spring. Their leaves have a large surface area to allow for maximum photosynthesis during their short growing season. A few deciduous plants keep their leaves all year round. These leaves have a protective wax covering similar to that of coniferous species' needles.

How to Use This Guide

This book offers a variety of information to help identify many of the common coniferous and deciduous trees found throughout the Pacific Northwest.

FAMILY
The guide lists each plant family, a grouping of one or more genera with similar overall characteristics. All pines, for instance, belong to the family Pinaceae, which includes several genera.

SPECIES NAMES
A scientific name and a common name are listed for each species. Every living organism has a unique scientific name that identifies the genus (a grouping of species with common characteristics) and the species. Occasionally names change as scientific information is discovered or reinterpreted. The most current or appropriate name is included in this book. Common names are those used in everyday conversation by people who live in an area where the species occur, so many plants have several common names. In this guide, the most widely accepted common name appears at the top of each entry with the species' scientific name.

OTHER NAMES
Additional common names and scientific names for the species are listed.

DESCRIPTION
To identify a species, use the photograph, data and written description together. Data on leaves, bark, cones, flowers, fruit and tree size accompany a description of the species.

HABITAT
Habitat is the type of environment in which a species normally grows. Many common plants are found in more than one habitat; some plants have more specific moisture requirements.

RANGE
Range is the geographic location where the species is known to grow.

NOTES
Notes on each species give special information, such as interesting features of the plant and traditional uses from eating to healing. These are intended as interesting details, not recommendations. Caution is advised in eating or using any wild plant.

SIMILAR SPECIES
Plants that are similar in appearance are identified in this section, along with range and extra information to help distinguish them from the species listed.

Rocky Mountain Juniper *Juniperus scopulorum*

DESCRIPTION
GENERAL Coniferous tree.
SIZE Normally to 33' (10 m) high; trunk to 12" (30 cm) in diameter; occasionally to 82' (25 m) high; trunk to 35" (90 cm) in diameter.
LEAVES Very small and scale-like on 4-sided twigs that resemble needles; mature leaves lack a glandular pit.
BARK Reddish brown to grayish brown, thin, fibrous, shredding continuously in flat-topped sections.

CONES Pollen cones small and normally on separate plants. Seed cones greenish, maturing to bluish purple, "berry" to 0.3" (8 mm) across with a heavy blue-gray bloom.

HABITAT
Normally found in dry, rocky areas at low to middle elevations in the mountains and along the coast; occasionally on riverbanks or lakeshores.

KEY FEATURES
Mature leaves lack a glandular pit on the back and have scale-like features that resemble the western redcedar. The cones are smooth with a bluish purple color.

Range.

Seed cones.

RANGE
Southern British Columbia east to Alberta and Colorado, south to New Mexico.

NOTES
The berry-like cones of this species require 2 years to mature. As a result, cones are always present on the same tree. The outer layer must be removed in order for the seeds to germinate. This occurs naturally when various birds and mammals feed on the berries and their digestive tracts remove the outer fleshy covering. Native peoples used the berries in a medicinal tea for stomach ailments.

SIMILAR SPECIES
Western Juniper *Juniperus occidentalis* grows to 30' (9 m) in height in central Washington southward to California. Its leaves are scale-like with a shallow glandular pit on the back, and its berry-like cones are bluish black.

Bark.

Western Redcedar *Thuja plicata*

OTHER NAMES
Also known as western red cedar, Pacific redcedar, giant cedar, arbor vitae and shingle-wood.

DESCRIPTION
GENERAL Coniferous tree.
SIZE Normally to 131' (40 m) high; trunk to 8' (2.4 m) in diameter; occasionally to 197' (60 m) high; trunk to 10' (3 m) in diameter.
LEAVES Evergreen; yellowish green, scale-like, flattened to 0.25" (6 mm) long in 4 rows on small twigs attached to vigorously growing branches.

BARK Reddish brown, thin and fibrous, forming long, narrow, flattened ridges as it ages. Can be torn off in very long strips.

CONES Pollen cones reddish and very small to 0.2" (4 mm) long. Seed cones greenish, brown when mature at 2 years. Cones are egg-shaped with 8–12 scales in woody, irregular clusters that drop during the winter months.

KEY FEATURES
The cones are egg-shaped. The leaves produce a characteristic scent when crushed. The bark of a mature tree is reddish brown.

Range.

Seed cones.

HABITAT
Primarily in moist to wet soils, in shaded forests; low to medium elevations.

RANGE
Alaska to NW California, east to the Rocky Mountains

NOTES

Western redcedar is well known for its decay-resistant properties, and it can live as long as 1,000 years. As a result, its wood makes excellent fence posts, pilings and siding. Trees that have fallen in the forest remain sound for hundreds of years. Many western redcedars, however, have substantial center rot, and become hollow near the ground. The largest western redcedar known measured at 21' (6.4 m) in diameter, making it the second largest native tree in diameter (the giant sequoia is the largest). This species is not among the tallest, however. Western redcedar is the provincial tree of British Columbia.

Bark.

Yellow Cypress *Callitropsis nootkatensis*

OTHER NAMES
Formerly *Chamaecyparis nootkatensis*, *Cupressus nootkatensis*; Incorrectly *Xanthocyparis nootkatensis*; Also known as Alaska yellow-cedar, Alaska cypress, Nootka cypress, Nootka false cypress and yellow cedar.

DESCRIPTION
GENERAL Coniferous tree.
SIZE Normally to 131' (40 m) high; trunk to 3' (90 cm) in diameter; occasionally to 164' (50 m) high; trunk to 5' (1.5 m) in diameter.

LEAVES Evergreen; Dull bluish green, flattened, scale-like to 0.25" (6 mm) long in 4 rows on small twigs attached to long branches.
BARK Brown and scaly when young, maturing to grayish brown with narrow intersecting fissures.

KEY FEATURES
Cones are rounded. Leaves produce a characteristic resinous scent when crushed. The bark of a mature tree is grayish brown. Inner bark is yellowish with a distinctive smell somewhat like raw potatoes.

Range.

Seed cones.

CONES Pollen cones are greenish yellow, growing to 0.16" (4 mm) long. Seed cones take 2 years to mature. During the first season they are greenish, round, knobby, berry-like spheres, brown when mature, with 4–6 woody scales. Good seed crops are produced every 4 or more years.

HABITAT
Moist to wet sites with plenty of moisture. Grows singly, in small clusters or in pure stands.

RANGE
Southeast Alaska south to the mountains of Oregon and NW California; sea level (in the north) to 7,000' (2,134 m) inland.

NOTES
The yellow cypress is an impressive slow-growing tree that commonly reaches the age of 1,000–1,500 years. The scent of yellow cypress is distinctive and its inner bark is said to smell like raw potatoes. Its wood is highly desirable, prized for custom interior finishing, millwork, boats and other uses. Native peoples used yellow cypress to carve canoe paddles and ceremonial masks.

Bark.

11

Incense Cedar *Calocedrus decurrens*

OTHER NAMES
Formerly *Libocedrus decurrens*; also known as California incense-cedar, pencil cedar, pecky cedar, bastard cedar, post cedar, white cedar.

DESCRIPTION
GENERAL Coniferous tree.

SIZE Normally to 49' (15 m) high; trunk to 5' (1.5 m) in diameter; occasionally to 151' (46 m) high; trunk to 7' (2.1 m) in diameter.

LEAVES Evergreen; scale-like; opposite in 4 rows with the side pair keeled; overlapping adjacent pairs; to 0.5" (1.2 cm) long.

BARK Reddish brown, thick, deeply furrowed and ridged.

CONES Pollen cones yellowish green, terminally on twigs; to 0.3" (7 mm) long. Seed cones green when young, brown when mature, hang downward; oblong in shape with 6 paired, hard, flattened scales; to 1" (2.5 cm) long. Cone crops are often light and there is wide variability of abundance within its range.

KEY FEATURES
Cones are oblong. Bark of the mature tree is reddish brown with deep furrows and ridges.

Range.

12

Seed cone.

HABITAT
Mountainous areas in mixed coniferous forests; low to high elevations.

RANGE
Mount Hood, Oregon, to NW Mexico.

NOTES
Incense cedar produces a dense understory that provides both cover and food for overwintering birds. Small mammals, including squirrels and chipmunks, benefit from the seeds of this tree. As this species ages, its growth pattern becomes more irregular, with an eccentric crown and a rapidly tapering trunk and buttressed base.

Bark of incense cedar.

This species is important in the manufacture of pencils, because its wood is very soft, does not splinter and can be sharpened in any direction.

SIMILAR SPECIES
Port Orford Cedar *Chamaecyparis lawsoniana* is a larger, less common species reaching 200' (60 m) in height and 4' (1.2 m) in diameter. The cones are tightly pressed against the branchlets and the foliage is flat—features that help to distinguish this species. Female cones have 8–10 scales. The range is very restricted, from SW Oregon to NW California.

13

Western White Pine *Pinus monticola*

OTHER NAMES
Also known as mountain white pine, Idaho white pine, silver pine.

DESCRIPTION

GENERAL Coniferous tree.

SIZE Normally to 100' (30 m) high; trunk to 3' (90 cm) in diameter; occasionally to 200' (60 m) high; trunk to 8' (2.4 m) in diameter.

LEAVES Evergreen; needles slender and flexible in bundles of 5; to 4" (10 cm) long. Mature bundles lack basal sheaths. No white lines on ventral surface of needles.

BARK Thin, smooth, grayish green when young; maturing to dark gray, broken into small, thick, rectangular, scaly plates separated with deep , longitudinal furrows and horizontal cracks.

CONES Pollen cones yellow, to 0.4" (1 cm) long. Seed cones yellow-green to purple, maturing to reddish brown; 12" (30 cm) long; elongated, slightly curved and pendulous (hang downward); scales thin, rounded, with dark tips that lack

KEY FEATURES
A 5-needle pine with needles to 4" (10 cm) long; curved cones to 12" (30 cm) long with dark tips on scales. Most pines in this area have needles approximately 2" (5 cm) long, with the exception of the whitebark pine (see p. 16) and the sugar pine (see p. 26), found in Oregon. The sugar pine cone, however, grows to 18" (45 cm) long, and its needles have white lines on the ventral surface.

Range.

Seed cone.

prickles; long-winged seeds. Good seed crops are produced every 3–4 years once trees reach 70 years. When cones mature, the seeds are shed and the cones fall during autumn and winter.

HABITAT
Thrives in a variety of sites: dry, sandy soils and rocky earth, peat bogs, gentle slopes and moist valleys.

RANGE
Southern British Columbia to central California, east to Montana.

NOTES
The western white pine is a large tree with a noticeably straight trunk and narrow, conical crown. Its presence often goes unnoticed in the woods until autumn, when its large seed cones are found on the forest floor.

Many Native peoples utilized this tree in a variety of ways. The bark was made into a tea for stomach disorders, rheumatism and tuberculosis. It was also applied externally to treat cuts and sores. Some groups used the pitch to treat stomach aches, coughs and sore throats, and others used pitch for waterproofing and cleansing. Women chewed the gum of the western white pine to make them more fertile. Its bark was used in making baskets and small canoes.

Bark.

Pollen cones.

Whitebark Pine *Pinus albicaulis*

OTHER NAMES
Also known as scrub pine, white pine, whitestem, alpine whitebark, pitch pine, scrub pine, creeping pine.

DESCRIPTION
GENERAL Coniferous tree.
SIZE To 50' (15 m) high; trunk to 2' (60 cm) in diameter.
LEAVES Evergreen; needles in bundles of 5; to 3.5" (9 cm) long; tend to be clustered toward the ends of the twigs.
BARK Whitish gray, smooth and thin, maturing to grayish brown to reddish brown, with narrow, loose, scaly plates.
CONES Pollen cones scarlet; to 0.6" (15 mm) long. Seed cones are purplish maturing to brown; to 3.3" (8 cm) long; permanently closed—do not open on drying; grow at right angles to the branch; often very pitchy; seed crops produced at irregular intervals; mature August to September.

HABITAT
Exposed slopes and ridges in subalpine zone to timberline; subalpine forests at altitudes from 3,000' (900 m) near the coast to 6.000' (1,800 m) inland.

RANGE
Central British Columbia to central California, east to Idaho and Wyoming.

KEY FEATURES
Very similar to limber pine, except for the cones. The pollen cones of whitebark pine are scarlet, and the seed cones are purplish and do not open even when lying on the ground.

Range.

Seed cones.

NOTES

Native people once gathered the cones and ate the large seeds of this pine. It is considered to be the most primitive native pine because its cones do not open until they decay on the ground. Whitebark pine seeds are an important food source for a wide variety of high-elevation birds and mammals, including Clark's nutcrackers, Steller's jays, ravens, pine grosbeaks, Williamson's sapsuckers, white-headed woodpeckers, hairy woodpeckers, red-breasted nutcrackers, white-breasted nuthatches, red crossbills, mountain chickadees, red squirrels, chipmunks, mice, voles, black bears and grizzly bears. Red squirrels are well known for storing whitebark pine cones in their middens. These middens in turn are often raided by grizzly bears, for which the cones are an extremely important food. The seeds are large and contain a high percentage of fat—a necessary nutrient for hibernating grizzly bears. Various problems, especially the infestation of the mountain pine beetle (*Dendroctonus ponderosae*) and the attack of white pine blister rust (*Cronartium ribicola*), have severely reduced the numbers of whitebark pine throughout its range.

Bark of old growth tree..

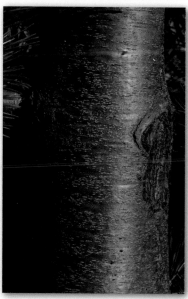

Bark of young tree..

17

Limber Pine *Pinus flexilis*

OTHER NAMES
Also known as Rocky Mountain white pine, white pine.

DESCRIPTION

GENERAL Coniferous tree.

SIZE Normally to 40' (12 m) high; trunk to 2' (60 cm) in diameter; occasionally to 50' (15 m) high; trunk to 36" (90 cm) in diameter.

LEAVES Evergreen; needles in bundles of 5; to 3.5" (9 cm) long; clustered at the ends of the branches giving them a bottle-brush-like appearance.

BARK Smooth, light gray, maturing to dark brown; thick, rough and furrowed into wide, scaly plates.

CONES Pollen cones small, yellow. Seed cones green, maturing to light brown; to 8.6" (22 cm) long; open while attached to the tree; unarmed; scales thick, rounded with a blunt point; good seed crops every 2–4 years.

KEY FEATURES
Very similar to whitebark pine, except for the cones. The pollen cones of limber pine are yellow and the seed cones are greenish, 2–3 times longer, and they open while still attached to the tree.

Range.

Seed Cone.

HABITAT
Dry, rocky exposed sites, including ridges and rocky slopes; foothills to subalpine.
RANGE
Southern British Columbia to New Mexico, east to Nebraska.
NOTES
The limber pine is a long-lived tree, known to survive for well over 1,000 years. Its scientific name, *flexilis*, refers to its very tough and flexible twigs, which can actually be twisted into knots. Plants living in exposed locations at timberline are shaped by the wind into crooked or twisted bonsai-like forms. The large seeds of this pine provide food for a variety of birds and mammals. In centuries past, they were also an important food for Native peoples and early pioneers.

Needles.

Bark.

Ponderosa Pine *Pinus ponderosa*

OTHER NAMES
Also known as bull pine, yellow pine, western yellow pine, rock pine.

DESCRIPTION
GENERAL Coniferous tree.
SIZE Normally to 90' (27 m) high; trunk to 3' (90 cm) in diameter; occasionally to 197' (60 m) high; trunk to 6' (1.8 m) in diameter.
LEAVES Evergreen; needles in bundles of 3 (occasionally 2, 4 or 5); to 11" (28 cm) long; edges sharply toothed.
BARK Dark gray, rough and scaly when young; mature specimens orange-brown to cinnamon, thick with deep fissures producing large, flat, flaky plates.
CONES Pollen cones reddish purple to yellow, to 1.2" (3 cm) long. Seed cones reddish -purple when young, brown when mature; to 6" (15 cm) long, with a sharp prickle near tip; in groups of 1–3; seed crops every 2–5 years.

HABITAT
Species forms open forests in hot, dry valleys at low elevations. It also forms mixed stands with Douglas-fir and western larch at eleva-

KEY FEATURES
Easy to identify by the 3 very long needles per bundle and the orange-brown bark of mature trees.

Range.

Pollen cone.

Seed cone.

tions reaching 4,920' (1,500 m).

RANGE

Southern British Columbia to New Mexico.

NOTES

Ponderosa pine is an important species in the wood industry, used to make door moldings, frames, paneling, cabinetwork and crates. It is not particularly long-lived compared with other conifers, rarely exceeding 400–600 years in age. On hot days, the older bark emits a vanilla-like aroma. The seeds of ponderosa pine provide food for many birds and small mammals, including grouse, quail and squirrels. This species is susceptible to severe damage by the mountain pine beetle.

The cambium (inner bark) from young trees was collected and eaten in the spring by several Native peoples. Chewing gum was made from lumps of the reddish pitch. Its resin was applied alone or in salves to abscesses, boils, carbuncles, rheumatic joints and aching backs. This pine has a long history of use by Aboriginal peoples and today it is still being used in construction.

Bark.

21

Lodgepole Pine *Pinus contorta*

OTHER NAMES
Also known as black pine, scrub pine, tamarack pine, mountain pine.

DESCRIPTION
GENERAL Coniferous tree.
SIZE Normally to 82' (25 m) high; trunk to 12" (30 cm) in diameter; occasionally to 131' (40 m) high; trunk to 3' (90 cm) in diameter.
LEAVES Evergreen; needles in bundles of 2; to 2.8" (7 cm) long.
BARK Thin, gray with a light covering of small, loose scales; coarse plates on mature specimens.
CONES Pollen cones reddish green to yellow, small; in clusters at branch tips in spring. Seed cones brown; to 2" (5 cm) long; hard, armed with prickles; usually paired, curved, pointing away from branch; usually remain closed and on the tree for 10–20 years; good crops every 1–3 years.

HABITAT
On a variety of sites ranging from rock outcrops to those with deep, rich organic soils; sea level to subalpine elevations.

KEY FEATURES
A 2-needle pine with cones that are usually paired, curved, pointing away from the branch.

Range.

Pollen cone.

Seed cones.

RANGE
Alaska to Oregon, east to Alberta.

NOTES
Three varieties of lodgepole pine are present. The shore pine *P. contorta* var *contorta* occurs along the coast as well as on dunes, bogs and rocky hilltops where poor growing conditions exist. In these habitats, this small tree often grows crooked and twisted to only 50' (15 m). Rocky Mountain lodgepole pine *P. contorta* var. *lalifolia* is found in the interior to the Rockies, where it grows straighter and taller, reaching 131' (40 m) high. These cones are normally closed with a resin bond; they only open when exposed to heat from a fire or direct sunlight.

The Sierra lodgepole pine (var. *murrayana*) ranges from the Cascade Mountains to northern Baja California. This variety is a tall, narrow tree with scaly bark, broad needles and symmetrical light-weight cones. It normally lives less than 300 years. When trees reach 100 to 140 years, they often fall victim to the mountain pine beetle. In the past, the harsh cold of the winters prevented the spread of this insect. The milder winters of recent years have left this pine more susceptible to the pine beetle in large areas of the North.

Bark.

Jack Pine *Pinus banksiana*

OTHER NAMES
Also known as Banksian pine, gray pine, scrub pine.

DESCRIPTION
GENERAL Coniferous tree.
SIZE Normally to 66' (20 m) high; trunk to 12" (30 cm) in diameter; occasionally to 80' (24 m) high; trunk to 24" (60 cm) in diameter.
LEAVES Evergreen; needles in bundles of 2; to 2" (5 cm) long.
BARK Thin, smooth, reddish brown to gray when young, maturing to dark brown, broken into thick, flaky plates separated with deep furrows.
CONES Pollen cones yellow to orange-brown; to 0.5" (1 cm) long; in clusters at ends of branches. Seed cones brown; to 3" (7.6 cm) long; hard and sometimes armed with prickles; usually paired, curved, tips point toward branch; usually remain closed and may remain on the tree for 10–20 years.

HABITAT
On sites with poor growing conditions; especially abundant in the boreal forest.

> **KEY FEATURES**
> A 2-needle pine with cones that are usually paired, curved, pointing toward the branch.

Range.

Seed cones.

RANGE
Alberta east to the Atlantic provinces.

NOTES
The fresh, juicy inner bark of the jack pine was eaten by some Native peoples. Male flowers were parboiled to remove excess resin and make them eatable. Pine needles were dried and pounded to make a powder for treating burns, blisters and cuts. Pine bark was boiled to make a medicinal tea for colds and flu. Pine bark tea was also combined with crowberries and given to people with coughs. Young jack pine is often browsed by deer and other mammals, causing trees to become deformed.

Pollen cones.

Bark.

Sugar Pine *Pinus lambertiana*

OTHER NAMES
Also known as big pine, great sugar pine.

DESCRIPTION
GENERAL Coniferous tree.

SIZE Normally to 164' (50 m) high; trunk to 6' (1.8 m) in diameter; occasionally to 246' (75 m) high; trunk to 11' (3.3 m) in diameter.

LEAVES Evergreen; needles in bundles of 5; to 4" (10 cm) long; needles have conspicuous white lines on ventral surface.

BARK Thin, grayish-green when young, maturing to red-brown or purple-brown large, elongated plates to 3" (7.5 cm) thick.

CONES Pollen cones yellow, to 0.6" (1.5 cm). Seed cones brownish; normally to 18" (45 cm) long occasionally to 21" (53 cm); pendulous (hang downward); scales thick and rounded with blunt points.

HABITAT
Mountainous areas; occurs in mixed coniferous forests.

RANGE
Oregon to California and northern Baja California, east to Nevada.

KEY FEATURES
Cones are very large (to 18"/45 cm long); needles have visible white lines on the ventral surface.

Range.

NOTES

The heartwood exudes sugar through wounds present on this aptly named pine. Some believe sugar pine tastes better than maple sugar. Unfortunately, its laxative properties allow only small quantities to be eaten at a time. This species may live as long as 800 years—if true, that is exceptional. The shape of its crown is unique, as several major limbs commonly reach far higher than its trunk. Some refer to this species as the "king of pines" because of its size and beauty. The large seeds were gathered by Native peoples for a food that was high in sugar.

Seed cone.

Needles..

Bark.

SIMILAR SPECIES

Western white pine (see p. 14) has smaller cones (to 11"/27 cm long); white lines not present on ventral surface of needles.

27

Western Larch *Larix occidentalis*

OTHER NAMES
Also known as western tamarack, tamarack, larch, mountain larch, hackmatack.

DESCRIPTION
GENERAL Coniferous tree.

SIZE Normally to 150' (46 m) high; trunk to 3' (90 cm) in diameter; occasionally to 230' (70 m) high; trunk to 6.6' (2 m) in diameter.

LEAVES Deciduous; needles in tufts of 15–30; 3-sided; to 2" (5 cm) long; shed for winter; needles are triangular in cross-section; twigs are slightly hairy.

BARK Thin, scaly, cinnamon brown when young, maturing to reddish brown, broken into thick, flaky plates separated with deep furrows.

CONES Pollen cones yellow; to 0.4" (1 cm) long. Seed cones reddish when young, brown when mature; to 1.6" (4 cm) long; erect; long bract tips extend beyond scales. Seed production begins as early as 15 years, and may

KEY FEATURES
A tall tree that normally occurs below 5,117' (1,560 m) with twigs that are only slightly hairy. Cones are large with visible bracts that project from beneath the scales.

Range.

Pollen cones.

continue for 200 years or more. Seeds produced in most years; good crops every 4–5 years.

HABITAT
Moist to dry sites, often gravelly or sandy; foothills to montane.

RANGE
British Columbia to Alberta and Montana, south to Oregon.

NOTES
The western larch is well known for providing exceptionally high-quality wood used in construction. Its bark contains Arabinogalactan, a water-soluble gum that has been used for offset lithography as well as in pharmaceuticals, cosmetics, ink products and paint. Galactan, a natural sugar found in the gum, resembles a bitter honey and has various uses in medicine.

Seed cones.

Bark.

29

Subalpine Larch *Larix lyallii*

OTHER NAMES
Also known as Alpine
larch, timberline larch.
DESCRIPTION
GENERAL Coniferous
tree.
SIZE Normally to 50'
(15 m) high; trunk to
12" (30 cm) in diame-
ter; occasionally to 82'
(25 m) high; trunk to 2'
(60 cm) in diameter.
LEAVES Deciduous;
needles in tufts of
15–40 on stubby twigs;
to 1.5" (3.8 cm) long;
needles are square in
cross-section. Twigs
are densely hairy.
BARK Thin, smooth,
grayish to yellowish
grey when young,
maturing to thick, red-
dish brown with large,
irregular scaly plates.
CONES Pollen cones
yellowish brown; small.
Seed cones purple
when young, dark brown when mature, to 2" (5 cm) long; erect. Scales
have matted white hairs on lower surface.
Bracts have elongated slender points that
extend beyond the scales.
HABITAT
At timberline; on rocky soils; extremely hardy.

KEY FEATURES
Young twigs are densely hairy. Cones
have bracts that extend beyond the
scales. Grows near timberline.

Range.

RANGE

British Columbia and SW Alberta to Oregon and NW Montana.

NOTES

Subalpine larch, like all larches, is well known for its bright yellow needles that are shed for winter. This often produces spectacular landscapes over large areas.

Native peoples used larches in several ways in their day-to-day lives. The gum was used as a baking powder. It was also applied to cuts and bruises, and chewed to relieve sore throats. Tea was brewed to treat colds, coughs and tuberculosis.

Mature seed cone.

Young seed cone.

Bark.

Tamarack *Larix laricina*

OTHER NAMES
Also known as Hackmatack, eastern larch, American larch, Alaska larch, juniper.

DESCRIPTION
GENERAL Coniferous tree.

SIZE Normally to 50' (15 m) high; trunk to 1' (30 cm) in diameter; occasionally to 82' (25 m) high; trunk to 2' (60 cm) in diameter.

LEAVES Deciduous; needles in tufts of 10–60; to 1" (2.5 cm) long, soft and very slender.

BARK Thin, smooth, gray when young, maturing to reddish brown, scaly.

CONES Pollen cones very small, egg-shaped. Seed cones red, pink, or yellowish-green when young, light brown when mature; to 0.75" (2 cm) long; erect.

HABITAT
Fens, sphagnum bogs and swamps; common across the northern boreal forest; low and medium elevations.

Range.

KEY FEATURES
Short needles and small cones with hidden bracts. Species prefers wet areas below timberline.

RANGE
Alaska east to Labrador, south to Minnesota.

NOTES
Tamarack was utilized by several Native groups for its medicinal properties. The fresh inner bark was used on burns and boils to bring out poisons and speed healing. The inner bark was used to stop bleeding and to treat hemorrhoids, earaches, inflamed eyes, jaundice and colic. A tea made from the inner bark was prepared to cleanse burns, treat gangrenous sores and stop itching. The leaves were also found to be useful in treating sore muscles, arthritis and diabetes. **Caution** is advised, however, as some people are allergic to species in this family, and the ingestion of tamarack needles may cause cramps and paralysis in some people.

Seed cone.

Bark.

33

White Spruce *Picea glauca*

OTHER NAMES
Also known as cat spruce, skunk spruce, pasture spruce, Canadian spruce.

DESCRIPTION
GENERAL Coniferous tree.

SIZE Normally to 66' (20 m) high; trunk to 1' (30 cm) in diameter; occasionally to 131' (40 m) high; trunk to 4' (1.2 m) in diameter.

LEAVES Evergreen; needles sharp-pointed, stiff, straight, spreading from all sides of branches (bottlebrush-like) or primarily on upper side of twig, to 0.8" (2 cm) long.

BARK Thin, smooth, gray or brown when young, maturing to dark gray or brown broken into irregular scales.

CONES Male and female cones on same tree. Pollen cones pale red; to 0.6" (1.5 cm) long.
Seed cones reddish purple when young, brown when mature; slender, cylindrical, hang downward; to 3.1" (8 cm) long.

KEY FEATURES
At well-drained sites at low to middle elevations. Cones are cylindrical, with rounded, smooth-edged scales.

Range.

34

Seed cone.

HABITAT
Grows best on well-drained, moist soils; from near sea level to timberline.

RANGE
Alaska and British Columbia east to Labrador, south to Maine, west to Minnesota; local in NW, Montana, South Dakota, Wyoming.

NOTES
The white spruce is a widespread conifer of Alaska and Canada west of the Cascades. It occurs in mixed stands, often with the trembling aspen.

In traditional Aboriginal cultures, the extremely pliable roots of this spruce were peeled and split to make rope or cord for lacing together the birch bark on canoes. The roots were also used to make finely woven baskets for several uses. Split roots were woven into watertight bags for cooking. The sap was used in a variety of ways. Skin problems were treated with direct applications of sap. Dried sap was chewed as a gum. Boiled pitch was taken in liquid form to relieve coughs and sore throats.

Needles.

Bark.

35

Black Spruce *Picea mariana*

OTHER NAMES
Also known as bog spruce, swamp spruce.

DESCRIPTION
GENERAL Coniferous tree.
SIZE Normally to 50' (15 m) high; trunk to 16" (40 cm) in diameter; occasionally to 98' (30 m) high; trunk to 2' (60 cm) in diameter.
LEAVES Evergreen; needles 4-sided, stiff, sharp-pointed; spreading on all sides of twig; to 0.6" (1.5 cm) long.
BARK Thin, scaly, reddish or grayish brown when young; maturing to dark gray with large, flaky scales.
CONES Pollen cones dark red, small. Seed cones reddish to purple when young, brown when mature; to 1.25" (3 cm) long. Seed cones remain on the tree for several years.

HABITAT
Bogs, swamps, upland sites near wetlands; also with jack pine or lodgepole pine and white spruce on upland sites; low to middle elevations.

KEY FEATURES
Trees often distorted. Species favors very wet areas. Cones small, purplish brown and spherical, and persist for many years.

Range.

Seed cone.

RANGE

Alaska and British Columbia east to Labrador, south to New Jersey, west to Minnesota.

NOTES

Clusters of cones often remain on the black spruce for up to 30 years. Fire greatly speeds up the gradual process of releasing seeds. Early European travelers found that the black spruce was a very important part of their survival in North America. Spruce beer was given every other day to the crew of Captain James Cook to prevent scurvy. Spruce beer is made by boiling the young growing tips of the branches in the spring and adding sugar, molasses and yeast.

Researchers have discovered that when starving caribou cows eat the tips of young black spruce branches, it causes them to abort their calves. This would aid the survival of the species, since it is unlikely that both the female and her young would survive in a starvation situation.

Immature seed cone.

Bark.

Sitka Spruce *Picea sitchensis*

OTHER NAMES
Also known as coast spruce, tideland spruce.

DESCRIPTION
GENERAL Coniferous tree.
SIZE Normally to 150' (45 m) high; trunk to 6.6' (2 m) in diameter; occasionally to 280' (84 m) high; trunk to 13' (3.9 m) in diameter.
LEAVES Evergreen; needles stiff, very sharp, flattened, slightly keeled below, bristling out in all directions from the twig; to 1.2" (3 cm) long.
BARK Thin, smooth, gray when young, maturing to dark reddish brown broken into large, loose, scaly plates.

CONES Pollen cones red; small. Seed cones reddish purple when young, light yellow to orange-brown when mature; to 4" (10 cm) long; pendulous. The scales are thin, irregular and wavy-edged.

HABITAT
Usually occurs along the Pacific coast, on low terraces of river floodplains; also found along inlets and borders of streams inland for about

KEY FEATURES
This coastal species favors wet sites. Cone scales are loose-fitting and wavy-edged.

Range.

Seed cone.

93 miles (150 km); low elevations to 1,640' (500 m).

RANGE

Southern Alaska and British Columbia to northern California; low to high elevations.

NOTES

Sitka spruce is a valuable species for both pulp and lumber. It produces high-grade lumber for many items, including boats, piano sounding boards and tops for musical instruments. Because of its light weight and outstanding strength, it was used in aircraft construction during both World Wars.

Like the other spruce species, the Sitka spruce was used for medicinal purposes by Native peoples. The pitch was used as medicine for gonorrhea, syphilis, colds, sore throats, internal swelling, rheumatism, and toothaches, and burns, boils, slivers and other skin irritations. The roots were used to make intricately woven watertight hats and baskets.

Immature seed cones.

Bark.

Englemann Spruce *Picea engelmannii*

OTHER NAMES
Also known as mountain spruce, Columbian spruce, silver spruce, white spruce.

DESCRIPTION
GENERAL Coniferous tree.
SIZE Normally to 131' (40 m) high; trunk to 3' (90 cm) in diameter; occasionally to 180' (55 m) high; trunk to 6' (1.8 m) in diameter.
LEAVES Evergreen; needles tend to curve toward upper side, sharp-pointed, slender, flexible; spread on all sides of twig; to 0.9" (2.4 cm) long.
BARK Thin, light brown to gray, broken into large, loose, coarse, rounded, brownish scales.
CONES Male and female cones on same tree. Pollen cones yellow to dark purple; to 0.6" (1.5 cm) long.
Seed cones reddish purple when young, brown when mature, cylindrical to narrowly ovoid, hanging; to 3" (7.6 cm) long. Cone scales loose-fitting, flexible, irregularly toothed, broadest near the middle, tapered to a toothed, split, blunt tip.

KEY FEATURES
The twigs are somewhat hairy. Cone scales loose-fitting, irregularly toothed, broadest near the middle, tapered to a toothed, split, blunt tip.

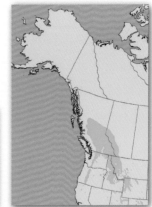

Range.

Seed cone.

HABITAT

Normally on mountain slopes at elevations of 3,300–9,800' (1,000–2,000 m), but is often found along streams farther down the mountains.

RANGE

Central British Columbia and SW Alberta, southeast to New Mexico (primarily in the Rocky Mountains).

NOTES

Trees are not normally considered edible, but several parts of various trees are. The young male catkins of Engelmann spruce are edible raw or cooked, and they can be used as a flavoring. Immature female cones are also edible if cooked, and the central portion is sweet and syrupy when roasted. The inner bark can be dried, then ground into a powder and used as a thickener in soups and other dishes. The seeds are edible raw, but they are small. The young shoot tips can be used to make a tea that is rich in vitamin C.

Bark.

41

Balsam Fir *Abies balsamea*

OTHER NAME
Also known as Canada balsam.

DESCRIPTION
GENERAL Coniferous tree.
SIZE Normally to 70' (21 m) high; trunk to 2' (60 cm) in diameter; occasionally to 82' (25 m) high; trunk to 28" (70 cm) in diameter.
LEAVES Evergreen; needles flat to 1" (2.5 cm) long; 2 or more lines of stomata (tiny pores used for gas exchange) in white bands beneath (a hand lens will help in viewing these).
BARK Thin, smooth, gray with resin blisters when young, maturing to brownish gray, irregular scales.
CONES Pollen cones yellow-red or purple-tinged, small. Seed cones erect, grayish brown when mature; to 4" (10 cm) long. Cones break up as early as August, leaving the bare axis on the tree for several years. Good seed every 2–4 years.

HABITAT
Boreal forest and moist woodlands; grows in pure stands or mixed woods.

RANGE
Northern Alberta east to the Atlantic provinces.

> **KEY FEATURES**
> Distinctive narrow, spire-like pyramidal crown and regular branching pattern.

Range.

Seed cones.

NOTES

Like all species of true fir, this one exhibits erect cones, and raised resin blisters are present on the bark of young true firs. The fragrant resin protects the tree from insects by rapidly flowing from any small or large openings on the tree prior to hardening. Its yellow resin is marketed as Canada balsam and is used in the preparation of microscope slides. This species is also a popular Christmas tree, grown on farms specifically for that market. Native peoples treated a variety of skin problems and infections with a salve or ointment made from the aromatic resin of the balsam fir. It was used externally to treat arthritis and internally for colds, coughs and asthma. Chest pains and gonorrhea were also treated with the resin.

Bark of young tree.

Bark of mature tree.

43

Subalpine Fir *Abies lasiocarpa*

OTHER NAMES
Also known as alpine fir, Rocky Mountain fir.

DESCRIPTION

GENERAL Coniferous tree, rocky mountain fir.

SIZE Normally to 75' (23 m) high; trunk to 16" (40 cm) in diameter; occasionally to 150' (45 m) high; trunk to 4' (1.2 m) in diameter.

LEAVES Evergreen; needles flat, to 1.5" (4 cm) long; needles do not lie flat on branch; white lines of stomata (tiny pores used for gas exchange) on upper and lower surfaces.

BARK Thin, smooth, ash gray blotched with raised resin blisters when young, maturing to irregular grayish brown scales.

CONES
Pollen cones are bluish and small. Seed cones are light to dark purple and grow to 4" (10 cm) long; erect with bracts dropping while still on the tree. Good cone crops occur about every 3 years.

KEY FEATURES
Needles have stomata (tiny pores used for gas exchange) on upper and lower surfaces; needles not flattened on branches; narrow crowns on trees.

Range.

Seed cones.

HABITAT
Normally at subalpine elevations (occasionally a stunted tree at treeline), but also found as low as sea level in the North.

RANGE
SE Alaska to New Mexico; sea level to 12,000' (3,658 m).

NOTES
The subalpine fir is an important tree for several species of wildlife. For grouse, the needles are an important food source. Deer, elk and bighorn sheep all feed on its bark, and various species of birds and mammals feed on the seeds it produces. The branches are short and sloped downwards, which helps this tree withstand heavy loads of snow and ice during the harsh winters.

This species, like most conifers, reproduces primarily by dropping its cones, and the seeds begin new trees. In northern coastal areas, though, it rarely produces cones. Instead, its populations are maintained primarily through layering, a process in which the lower branches produce new roots.

Bark.

Amablis Fir *Abies amabilis*

OTHER NAMES
Also known as Cascades fir, Pacific silver fir.

DESCRIPTION
GENERAL Coniferous tree.

SIZE Normally to 100' (30 m) high; trunk to 35" (90 cm) in diameter; occasionally to 180' (55 m) high; trunk to 4' (1.2 m) in diameter.

LEAVES Evergreen; needles flat to 1.5" (4 cm) long; most are notched at the tip, with two or more white lines of stomata (tiny pores used for gas exchange) underneath; needles lie flat on branch and those on upper side of twig point forward.

BARK Thin, smooth, ash gray with chalky white blotches and resin blisters when young, maturing to reddish gray or reddish brown, broken into scaly plates.

CONES Pollen cones are reddish. Seed cones are dark purple and erect, and grow to 5" (12.5 cm) long; bracts fall apart while still on the tree, leaving a "spike" standing on the tree.

KEY FEATURES
Needles lie flat on branch; those on upper side of twig point forward; seed cones deep purple.

Range.

Seed cone.

HABITAT
Normally in moist forests with well-drained soils; grows in pure stands or mixed with other conifers; sea level to 6,000' (1,829 m) elevation.

RANGE
SE Alaska south to California.

NOTES
The wood of the Amabilis fir is used for pulpwood, plywood and general construction lumber. This fir grows extremely slowly and requires up to 100 years to reach sufficient size to be used for lumber. A tree 2' (60 cm) in diameter is likely over 200 years old. *Amabilis* means "lovely," an appropriate name for this beautiful conifer. Native peoples chewed the pitch of various firs (*Abies* spp.) for enjoyment.

Bark.

Cones fall apart while on the tree.

Grand Fir *Abies grandis*

OTHER NAMES
Also known as lowland white fir, lowland fir, white fir, silver fir, yellow fir, stinking fir.

DESCRIPTION
GENERAL Coniferous tree.

SIZE Normally to 131' (40 m) high; trunk to 3' (90 cm) in diameter; occasionally to 266' (81 m) high; trunk to 61" (1.5 m) in diameter.

LEAVES Evergreen; needles flat to 2" (5 cm) long; needles blunt; needles lie flat on branch; two lines of stomata (tiny pores used for gas exchange) on lower surface.

BARK Thin, smooth, grayish brown with white mottling and numerous resin blisters when young, maturing to deep brown, broken into thick, irregular furrows with flat ridges.

CONES Pollen cones are yellowish and small. Seed cones yellowish green to green, erect, growing to 4.75" (12 cm) long. The scales

KEY FEATURES
Present in low-lying areas; needles long and blunt, two lines of white dots on lower surface only.

Range.

Seed cone.

are much wider than long, and the scales and seeds fall off the cone as they mature. This species produces fewer seeds than other firs.

HABITAT

In low-lying areas with other tree species; occasionally in pure stands; low to middle elevations.

RANGE

Southern British Columbia south to California, east to Montana and Idaho.

NOTES

The grand fir obtained its common name from its great height. It has a long history of use by Native peoples. The resin gum was used for its healing properties and as a glue. The bark was used to make canoes. The knots were carefully shaped by steaming and carving, and made into halibut hooks and other fishing hooks. The bark was boiled with stinging nettles and the decoction was used for bathing and as a general tonic. A medicinal tea for colds was brewed from the needles. The bark of the grand fir was crushed along with the bark of red alder and western hemlock and made into an infusion that was drunk for internal injuries.

Bark.

Noble Fir *Abies procera*

OTHER NAMES
Also known as red fir, white fir.

DESCRIPTION
GENERAL Coniferous tree.
SIZE Normally to 200' (60 m) high; trunk to 5' (1.5 m) in diameter; occasionally to 295' (90 m) high; trunk to 9' (2.75 m) in diameter.
LEAVES Evergreen; needles 4-sided, narrow, to 1.5" (4 cm) long; with conspicuous groove along the upper surface and 1 or 2 white rows of stomata (tiny pores used for gas exchange) above, and 2 rows below; needles twisted upward in such a way that the lower surface of the branch is exposed.
BARK Smooth, grayish brown with resin blisters when young, maturing to brown, scaly, longitudinal plates that easily flake off.
CONES Pollen cones are reddish. Seed cones are green, changing to purplish brown at maturity, erect, hard and growing to 7" (18 cm) long. The bracts are sharp-pointed and prominent, nearly hiding the scales. Squir-

KEY FEATURES
Found only in mid-mountain slopes of the Washington Cascades. Cone is large, shingled and spiny.

Range.

Seed cones.

rels sometimes cut the large, heavy cones of this species and drop them to the ground—a dangerous situation for those below!

HABITAT

Moist soils from mid- to upper-elevation coniferous forests; associated with other conifers, especially amabilis fir; not found in pure stands.

RANGE

Washington south to NW California

NOTES

This fir is well named—truly a noble species. It is the largest of the true firs and its appearance is often rated as magnificent. Some amazing stands of this handsome species can be found at middle elevations in the Cascades of Washington. This is an exceptionally long-lived tree. Some specimens can reach the age of 1,000 years.

Bark of young tree.

Bark of mature tree.

Douglas-fir *Pseudotsuga menziesii*

OTHER NAMES
Also known as common Douglas-fir, green Douglas-fir.

DESCRIPTION
GENERAL Coniferous tree.

SIZE Normally to 200' (60 m) high; trunk to 9' (2.7 m) in diameter; occasionally to 295' (90 m) high; trunk to 15' (4.5 m) in diameter.

LEAVES Evergreen; needles flat; often appearing to be flattened in 2 rows; to 1.2" (3 cm) long; smell of camphor when crushed.

BARK Thin, smooth, grayish brown with resin blisters when young; maturing to dark brown, broken with deep, reddish brown, rough vertical fissures.

CONES Pollen cones yellow to orange-red, catkin-like; to 0.8" (2 cm) long. Seed cones erect, green to purple or red when young, yellowish brown to purplish brown when mature; to 3.5" (9 cm) long; bracts prominent and 3-pronged (pitchfork) shape.

HABITAT
Variable from moist to very dry sites; foothills to subalpine; commonly found with other conifers.

RANGE
Central British Columbia and Alberta to New Mexico.

KEY FEATURES
Cones are present year–round, with prominent, visible bracts with a 3-pronged (pitchfork) shape.

Range.

Seed cones at various stages of development.

NOTES

This species was first described as a pine, hemlock and fir. Eventually, in 1791, Archibald Menzies placed it in its own genus, *Pseudotsuga*, meaning "false hemlock." This species has been known to survive for over 1,300 years. There are two subspecies: coastal Douglas-fir *P. menziesii* ssp. *menziesii* and interior Douglas-fir *P. menziesii* var. *glauca*. Coastal Douglas-fir occurs primarily west of the Cascade and Coast mountains, while interior Douglas-fir is found east of these ranges. Interior Douglas-fir is distinguished by its bluish-green needles and smaller cones—to 3.2" (8 cm) long—while the cones of coastal Douglas-fir are longer than 4" (10 cm).

Like so many other tree species, this one was used in various ways by Native people for food and well-being. The seeds provided food to several groups. In certain climatic conditions, a crystalline sugar is produced on the branches in early summer, which was harvested as food. The sap was also chewed to relieve cold symptoms.

A legend nicely explains the presence of the 3-pronged bracts that are so prominent on the cones of only the Douglas-fir. Deer mice are friends of the Douglas-fir, and the cones help them hide from their enemy, the fox. Since the mouse is a wee bit too large to fit inside the cone completely, the hind feet and tail of the mouse are visible while it hides.

Bark of old growth tree.

53

Western Hemlock *Tsuga heterophylla*

OTHER NAMES
Also known as Pacific hemlock, west coast hemlock.

DESCRIPTION
GENERAL Coniferous tree.

SIZE Normally to 160' (50 m) high; trunk to 3.3' (1 m) in diameter; occasionally to 197' (60 m) high; trunk to 4' (1.2 m) in diameter.

LEAVES Evergreen; needles to 1" (2.5 cm) long; irregularly spaced, unequal in length; lay flat on branch.

BARK Scaly, reddish brown to grayish brown when young, maturing to dark brown, broken into thick, flat plates separated with deep furrows.

CONES Pollen cones yellow; to 0.2" (4 mm) long. Seed cones purplish green when young, light brown when mature; to 1" (2.5 cm) long with few scales; oblong in shape, mature in a single season and drop during winter.

HABITAT
In a variety of soils; requires plentiful moisture; occasionally grows in pure stands but usually mixed with other tree species; very common at low to middle elevations.

KEY FEATURES
A drooping tree tip quickly identifies a hemlock from a distance. Leaves are irregularly spaced, lay flat on branch. Cones are small with few scales.

Range.

RANGE

Southern Alaska to NW California along the Pacific coast; SE British Columbia and Alberta to northern Idaho and NW Montana in the Rocky Mountains.

Seed cone.

NOTES

The western hemlock is a common species found at low to middle elevations. Its lumber is used for windows, doors, staircases and moldings, and in general construction. If the needles are crushed, they have an odor similar to a European weed called hemlock, hence this species' common name. The scientific name *heterophylla* means "variable leaves"— one of the best identifying features for this species. Native peoples often utilized the soft cambium layer as food in springtime. Western hemlock was also valued for use in the preparation of dyes and for tanning hides and making carvings, bedding, fish hooks and waterproofing material. Medicinal uses included poultices, chest liniments for colds, a salve to prevent sunburn (when mixed with deer tallow), and a tea (made from the bark, along with cascara and red alder bark) for hemorrhaging and internal injuries.

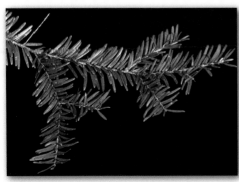

Needles.

Bark.

Mountain Hemlock *Tsuga mertensiana*

OTHER NAME
Also known as black hemlock.

DESCRIPTION

GENERAL Coniferous tree.

SIZE Normally to 50' (15 m) high; trunk to 20" (51 cm) in diameter; occasionally to 100' (30 m) high; trunk to 3' (90 cm) in diameter.

LEAVES Evergreen; needles to 2" (5 cm) long; most are equal in length on a twig; grow in all directions around branch.

BARK Thin, rough, brown when young, maturing to gray or dark brown, flat-topped ridges with furrows.

CONES Pollen cones bluish to 0.2" (4 mm) long. Seed cones light to dark purple when young, brown when mature; to 3" (7.5 cm) long; cylindrical and pendulous (hang downward); fall to the ground intact during spring or early summer after releasing their seeds during the winter months.

HABITAT
In the deep, moist soils of the subalpine at altitudes to 900' (1,800 m). In pure stands or with other conifers including alpine fir, Engelmann spruce, subalpine larch, whitebark pine

KEY FEATURES
A common species in the subalpine. Leaves grow in all directions around branch. Cone is twice as long as that of the western hemlock.

Range.

Seed cone.

and Amabilis fir.

RANGE

SE Alaska to central California along the Pacific Coast; SE British Columbia to northeast Oregon in the Rocky Mountains.

NOTES

Mountain hemlock closely resembles western hemlock (see p. 54), but grows at higher elevations and appears darker and somewhat denser in a hemlock forest. During the winter, mountain hemlock is often blanketed with over 20' (6 m) of snow in its subalpine environment. This insulating blanket often will keep the roots just above freezing temperature, enabling the tree to grow year-round. This species is not as shade tolerant as western hemlock and as a result it often becomes the dominant species. Unlike most conifers, the mountain hemlock may have some branches growing upwards from the trunk, which makes it useless for shelter in the rain.

Indian paint fungus (*Echinodontinum tinctorium*) is one polypore that is known to infect both hemlock species as well as firs. It attacks both live and dead trees, causing an extensive white heart rot in its host.

Needles.

Bark.

Western Yew *Taxus brevifolia*

OTHER NAMES
Also known as Pacific yew, mountain mahogany.

DESCRIPTION
GENERAL Coniferous tree.
SIZE Normally to 15' (4.5 m) high; trunk to 6" (15 cm) in diameter; occasionally to 45' (13.5 m) high; trunk to 12" (30 cm) in diameter.
LEAVES Evergreen; needle-like; dark green above, light green below; to 1.2" (3 cm) long; needles lie flat on branches.
BARK Thin, rose red when young, maturing to thin, reddish brown to purplish brown; and scale-like.
CONES Male and female cones on separate trees. Pollen cones yellow; round clusters of stamens to 0.1" (3 mm) across. Seed-bearing fruit is "berry-like," cup-shaped, greenish when young, scarlet when mature; to 0.4" (9 mm) across.

HABITAT
Moist mature forest, common along the coast; low to middle elevations.

KEY FEATURES
A scarlet berry-like "fruit" is produced rather than a cone. Needles appear in flat sprays.

Range.

Flowers.

RANGE
Southern Alaska to Idaho, south to California.
NOTES
The needle-like leaves of this coni-fer remain on the tree for about 8 years. Originally considered a "trash tree" in logging operations, this species has achieved worldwide fame for taxol, a chemical that is produced from its bark. Taxol has been successfully used to treat certain cancers, including breast and ovar-ian cancers. The bark was harvested in spring and early summer when sap flow made it easier to peel off. A total of 10 large yew trees were required for a single 2-gram treatment. Today a fungus is cultivated to produce taxol for cancer treatments.

Seed cone.

Bark.

Bigleaf Maple *Acer macrophyllum*

OTHER NAMES
Also known as broad-leaf maple, Oregon maple.

DESCRIPTION
GENERAL Deciduous tree.

SIZE Normally to 80' (24 m) high; trunk to 12" (30 cm) in diameter; occasionally to 115' (35 m) high; trunk to 40" (1 m) in diameter.

LEAVES Simple, opposite, deciduous; divided, deeply notched with 5 lobes; to 10" (25 cm) long: occasionally to 24" (60 cm).

BARK Thin, smooth and green when young, maturing to grayish brown, furrowed with narrow ridges.

FLOWERS Greenish yellow to pale yellow; to 0.1" (3 mm) across; numerous on short stalks in a raceme (hanging cylindrical cluster); pollen flowers and seed flowers occur together in same cluster, appearing before the leaves have expanded.

FRUIT In pairs, each with wings; to 2.5" (1 cm) long; swollen hairy seed; forming large clusters; to 60° apart from one another.

KEY FEATURES
Leaf indented more than halfway between lobes. Stiff hairs are found on the fruit.

Range.

Flower raceme.

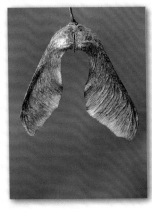

Winged fruit.

HABITAT
Favors coarse, gravelly, moist soils and newly disturbed sites; at low to middle elevations.

RANGE
SW British Columbia to southern California along the Pacific coast, inland to the Cascades.

NOTES
Massive amounts of epiphytic mosses, liverworts, ferns and other plants are often present on the bark and limbs of this maple. Water is absorbed by the bark, creating an ideal growing environment for these

Leaf.

epiphytes (plants that grow on other plants). Researchers have found that the bigleaf maple produces "canopy roots" to share the nutrients that are stored in these plant masses. The bark was traditionally used to treat sore throats, and to treat tuberculosis. The wood was used to make canoe paddles. The sap can be gathered to make a sweet syrup—although much less sweet than sugar maple. The fragrant, sweet-tasting flowers make beautiful garnishes for salads and cakes. Wood from the bigleaf maple is used in making furniture, flooring, interior paneling, guitars and other items.

Bark of young tree.

Bark of mature tree.

61

Douglas Maple *Acer glabrum*

OTHER NAME
Also known as Rocky Mountain maple.

DESCRIPTION

GENERAL Deciduous tree or tall shrub.

SIZE To 33' (10 m) high; trunk to 10' (25 cm) in diameter.

LEAVES Simple, opposite, deciduous; double-toothed, divided into 3–5 lobes to 5.5" (14 cm) long.

BARK Thin, smooth, grayish brown when young, maturing to brown with a rough surface.

FLOWERS Yellowish green; to 0.2" (5 mm) across; numerous on short stalks in drooping clusters; flowers appear with unfolding leaves; pollen and seed flowers found on separate trees.

FRUIT In pairs, each with wings; to 1" (2.5 cm) long; often rose-colored, turning brown in autumn; seed section is strongly wrinkled; to 45° apart from one another.

HABITAT
Grows along streams and similar moist sites as well as cliffs, bluffs and ledges; at low to middle elevations.

KEY FEATURES
A shrub-like tree with fruit wings that are often red-tinged in summer and strongly wrinkled.

Range.

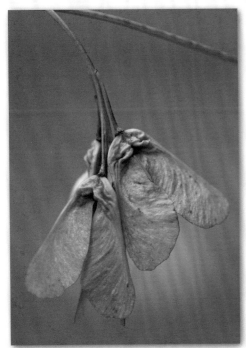

Winged fruit.

RANGE
Alaska to New Mexico, west to Alberta and Montana.

NOTES
This species often grows in a shrub-like form with an irregular and uneven crown. Its very colourful red and crimson autumn foliage makes it suitable as an ornamental in small gardens. This tree is very similar to the bigleaf maple.

Bark.

Leaf.

Vine Maple *Acer circinatum*

OTHER NAME
Also known as mountain maple.

DESCRIPTION
GENERAL Deciduous tree or small shrub.
SIZE To 33' (10 m) high; trunk to 6" (15 cm) in diameter.
LEAVES Simple, opposite, deciduous; divided into 7–9 double-toothed lobes; nearly circular in shape; to 6" (15 cm) long. The dark green color often changes to shades of yellow and red in summer. Autumn brings even more intense red and yellow colors.
BARK Thin, smooth, green when young, maturing to bright reddish brown, sometimes marked with shallow crevices.
FLOWERS Purple or red sepals and white petals; to 0.5" (1.2 cm) across; in loose drooping clusters; male and female organs in the same flower, but only male or female organs are functional in each cluster.

KEY FEATURES
Leaf with 7–9 lobes; flower has red or purple sepals with white petals; wing angle approximately 180°.

Range.

Flower.

Winged fruit.

FRUIT In pairs, each with wings; to 1.5" (4 cm) long; bright red in summer when ripe; seed portion swollen, hairless; seed wings spread to 180° apart from one another.

HABITAT
Common understory species found along stream banks, forest openings and disturbed areas; at low to middle elevations.

RANGE
Central British Columbia to California.

NOTES
The vine maple normally has a crooked trunk with several spreading limbs that support an irregular crown.
Native peoples carved spoons, bowls, platters and other small household utensils from the wood of this species.

Bark.

Leaf.

Paper Birch *Betula papyrifera*

OTHER NAMES
Also known as canoe birch, silver birch, white birch.

DESCRIPTION
GENERAL Deciduous tree.
SIZE Normally to 100' (30 m) high; trunk to 16" (40 cm) in diameter; occasionally to 131' (40 m) high; trunk to 30" (75 cm) in diameter.
LEAVES Simple, alternate, deciduous; pale green, turning yellow in autumn; ovate with a pointed tip; margins doubly toothed; to 4" (10 cm) long.
BARK Thin, smooth, reddish to coppery brown when young, often maturing to creamy white but may remain reddish, with conspicuous dark horizontal lines (lenticels); frequently sheds in large sheets.
FLOWERS Male and female catkins present on the same tree, female catkins shorter and thinner than male catkins; to 1.6" (4 cm) long.
FRUIT Mature seed catkins with nutlets inside; catkins to 1.5" (3.8 cm) long; break apart when ripe.

HABITAT
Thrives in a variety of forests, usually on moist, well-drained sites as well as around bogs and other wetlands; also a pioneer species in burned areas; at low to middle elevations.

KEY FEATURES
Leaves ovate with a pointed tip. Bark of mature trees sheds in large sheets.

Range.

Seed catkin.

Pollen catkins in winter condition.

RANGE

NW Alaska to Oregon; east to Newfoundland south to New York.

NOTES

The thin, peeling bark of the white birch is renowned for its use in making birchbark canoes and ornaments. Native peoples also used the leaves of this tree to make soap and shampoo. The sap was used as a tonic for colds and can also be used to make vinegar or beer. Syrup can be made from birch sap, but 20–26 gallons (80–100 L) of sap are needed to make one quart (1 L) of syrup!

Research is currently being conducted on the anti-tumor activity of betulinic acid, a compound that makes birchbark white, and which may prove useful in the treatment or prevention of skin cancer.

Bark.

SIMILAR SPECIES

Alaska Paper Birch ***Betula neoalaskana*** occurs from Alaska to northern British Columbia east to Ontario; twigs are densely covered with yellowish bumpy resin glands.

Water Birch *Betula occidentalis*

OTHER NAMES
Also known as black birch, mountain birch, western birch, red birch, river birch.

DESCRIPTION
GENERAL Deciduous tall shrub or tree.
SIZE Normally to 20' (6 m) high; trunk to 6" (15 cm) in diameter; occasionally to 50' (15 m) high; trunk to 14" (35 cm) in diameter.
LEAVES Simple, alternate, deciduous; deep yellowish green turning yellowish brown in autumn; broadly ovate with a sharp point; margins doubly toothed; to 2" (5 cm) long.
BARK Thin, smooth, shiny, dark reddish brown with long, horizontal white lenticels; does not peel as the paper birch does.

FLOWERS
Male and female catkins present on the same tree and at same time

or earlier as leaves; female catkins erect; male catkins drooping; to 2.4" (6 cm) long.
FRUIT Mature seed catkins hanging with nutlets inside; catkins to 1.6" (4 cm) long; break apart when ripe.

HABITAT
Grows best in moist areas including streams, springs, marshes, lakes; often present in slightly saline sites; low to middle elevations.

RANGE
Alaska to Manitoba, south to California; east of the Cascades

NOTES
This species normally grows to a tall shrub and under favorable conditions will reach tree status. It is commonly found with several trunks growing from a central source beside water.

Natives traditionally harvested sap from hollowed-out cavities and made a sweet drink. Like all birch, the water birch was used for firewood because of the high content of pitch in the bark.

KEY FEATURES
Leaves are small with only 4–5 veins per side; brown bark does not peel; wart-like reddish glands on the branchlets.

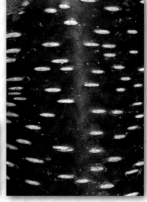

Bark.

Mountain Alder *Alnus incana tenuifolia*

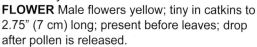

OTHER NAMES
Also known as *A. tenui-folia*; thinleaf alder, river alder.

DESCRIPTION
GENERAL Deciduous tree or large shrub.
SIZE Normally to 30' (9 m) high; trunk to 6" (15 cm) in diameter; occasionally to 40' (12 m) high; trunk to 12" (30 cm) in diameter.
LEAVES Deciduous; ovate to elliptical: to 4" (10 cm) long; double-toothed with wavy lobes; 6–9 straight, parallel veins run to the edge on each side.
BARK Thin, smooth, grayish-green when young, maturing to reddish gray and scaly.

FLOWER Male flowers yellow; tiny in catkins to 2.75" (7 cm) long; present before leaves; drop after pollen is released.
Female flowers become narrow green cones maturing to brown; cone to 0.25" (6 mm) long; present in clusters of 3–9 cones. Flowers before leaves are present.
FRUIT Nutlet is narrowly winged, inside cone; remains on tree during summer until the following spring.

HABITAT
Banks of streams, swamps, similar areas with moist soils.
RANGE
Central Alaska to California and Arizona; generally at interior sites west of the Cascades.
NOTES
This aptly named species is generally found in the mountains and interior. Native peoples once made a red dye from the powdered bark and also used the bark in the treatment of rheumatic fever. The bark contains salicin, now used as a standard prescribed medicine for this disease.

KEY FEATURES
Double-toothed leaves with wavy lobes that are not inrolled; present east of the Cascades.

Bark.

69

Red Alder *Alnus rubra*

OTHER NAMES
Also known as Oregon alder, western alder.

DESCRIPTION

GENERAL Deciduous tree.

SIZE Normally to 82' (25 m) high; trunk to 2' (60 cm) in diameter; occasionally to 100' (30 m) high; trunk to 2.5' (80 cm) in diameter.

LEAVES Deciduous; dark green above; ovate to elliptical; to 5" (12.5 cm) long; the dull teeth form rounded lobes; outer margin is slightly turned under; 8–15 straight, parallel veins run to the edge on each side.

BARK Thin, smooth, gray when young, maturing to brown with patches of white lichens and may become slightly scaly; fresh wounds reveal inner bark and red heartwood.

FLOWER Pollen catkins in small clusters at shoot tips; male yellowish to 6" (15 cm) long; female reddish to 0.5" (1.2 cm) long and very narrow; catkins are present before leaves appear.

FRUIT Nutlet inside cone-like structure; green cones mature to brown in clusters; cones to 0.5" (1.3 cm) long; nutlet bordered by very narrow wings.

KEY FEATURES
Round-lobed leaves with leaf margin rolled under; present west of the Cascades; blotches of white lichen cover the bark's surface.

Range.

Female catkins.

Fruit.

HABITAT
Moist areas: along streams, valley bottoms and floodplains; open areas.

RANGE
SE Alaska to central California, generally west of the Cascades.

NOTES
Alder species can be difficult to identify. Positive identification relies upon several characteristics, and species are known to hybridize where their ranges overlap. Female alder catkins ripen into woody, cone-like structures (in clusters), which contain tiny nutlets between the woody bracts.

Red alder is normally a short-lived tree that provides a fast-growing cover for various conifers to take root. The roots are shallow and wide-spreading like those of legumes, often with swellings or nodules that contain nitrogen-fixing bacteria. These bacteria enrich the soil by converting nitrogen from the air into chemicals that plants can use. Native people used the inner bark to make a reddish dye. The buds and catkins provide food for ruffed grouse.

Leaf.

Bark.

71

Green Alder *Alnus viridis crispa*

OTHER NAMES
Also known as *A. crispa, A. crispa crispa*.
DESCRIPTION
GENERAL Deciduous tree or shrub.
SIZE Normally to 10' (3 m) high; occasionally to 30' (9 m) high.
LEAVES Deciduous; ovate to elliptic; yellowish green on upper surface, with small and distinctly sharp teeth; single or double-toothed; to 3.2" (8 cm) long.
BARK Thin, smooth, grayish brown.
FLOWER Male flowers yellow-green; tiny; catkins sessile; groups of 3–6 in drooping clusters; catkins to 3.25" (8 cm) long. Female flowers in stalked catkins; catkins woody, to 6" (15 cm) long; male and female flowers appear before unfolding leaves, remain on branch during winter.

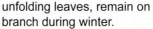

FRUIT Seed cones brown when mature with broad-winged nutlets, each to 0.1" (2 mm) long; shed from cone-like catkins.
HABITAT
Open moist woods, wetlands and streams.
RANGE
Central Alaska to Newfoundland, north past treeline to Arctic coast south to Colorado; east of the Rocky Mountain Trench.
NOTES
Alder was a preferred wood for Aboriginal peoples, who used it for smoking meats, salmon and other fish because of the wonderful flavor it gave the food. It was also used in the preparation of tanning hides, and soaked in water to make snowshoes. Alder bark tea was used to treat hemorrhoids.

> **KEY FEATURES**
> Leaves small with sharp teeth, single or double-toothed.

Bark.

Sitka Alder *Alnus viridis sinuata*

OTHER NAMES
Also known as *A. sinuata*, *A. crispa sinuata*; mountain alder, wavyleaf alder.

DESCRIPTION
GENERAL Deciduous tree or tall shrub.
SIZE Normally to 30' (9 m) high; trunk to 6" (15 cm) in diameter; occasionally to 49' (15 m) high; trunk to 8' (20 cm) in diameter.
LEAVES Deciduous; ovate and shallowly wavy-lobed; to 3" (7.5 cm) long; double-toothed with long-pointed teeth; 6–10 straight, parallel veins run to the edge on each side.
BARK Thin, smooth, grayish green with light-colored, warty horizontal lenticels.
FLOWER Male flowers tiny and yellowish; numerous without stalks forming catkins; catkins to 5.25" (13 cm) long. Female flowers reddish; narrow cone-like catkins to 0.4" (1 cm) long; appear with unfolding leaves.

FRUIT Seed cones brown when mature with broad-winged nutlets, cone to 0.5" (1.3 cm) long; 3–6 cones clustered on a long stalk; shed from cone-like catkins; seed cones not present in winter.
HABITAT
Moist sites: along streams, near lakes or wet meadows.

RANGE
Southern Alaska to California; east to Alberta and Colorado.
NOTES
This tree is closely related to the Green Alder *Alnus viridis crispa* (p. 72). It is distinguished by its cones, leaves and flowering characteristics.
SIMILAR SPECIES
White Alder *Alnus rhombifolia* forms a tree to 9 m (30') high in Washington and southward. This alder grows along streams in sagebrush country, normally west of the Cascade Mountains.

KEY FEATURES
Fringe-like (wavy) leaf margins are unique to this tree; seed cones not present in winter.

Bark.

Pacific Willow *Salix lucida lasiandra*

OTHER NAMES

Formerly *S. lancifolia, S. lasiandra*; also known as yellow willow, whiplash willow, red willow, golden willow, caudate willow, black willow, western black willow.

DESCRIPTION

GENERAL Deciduous tree or tall shrub.

SIZE Normally to 36' (11 m) high; trunk to 12" (30 cm) in diameter; occasionally to 60' (18 m) high; trunk to 24" (60 cm) in diameter.

LEAVES Simple, alternate, deciduous; shiny green above and whitish below; lance-shaped with a round base; fine-toothed margin; usually twisted to one side; to 5.25" (13 cm) long. Leaf-stems with glands at base of leaf.

BARK Thin, gray to dark brown when young, maturing to blackish, rough with furrows or fissures.

FLOWERS Catkins to 4" (10 cm) long, with hairy, yellow or brown scales; appear with leaves in spring.

FRUIT Reddish brown, hairless capsules; to 0.25" (6 mm) long; maturing early summer.

KEY FEATURES

A tree-sized willow displaying leafstems with glands at base of leaf.

Range.

Leaves.

HABITAT
Grows best along rivers, streams and lakes, and in valleys.

RANGE
Central Alaska east to Sas-katchewan; south to southern New Mexico and southern California; to 8,000' (2,438 m).

NOTES
Few willows reach the size of a tree. This is one species that does, along with the peachleaf willow (see Similar Species, below), which may also be encountered in the Pacific Northwest. It is often difficult, however, to distinguish closely related species.

All species of willows produce a chemical called salicin, related to acetyl-salicylic acid (ASA)—also known as aspirin. This is likely the reason many Aboriginal peoples used various preparations from willows to treat toothache, stomach ache, diarrhea and dysentery. Willow stems were also commonly used for basketry and bow making, and the bark was also important in fabric making.

Bark.

SIMILAR SPECIES
Peachleaf Willow *Salix amygdaloides* is a tree-sized willow displaying leafstems without glands at base of leaf and leaves that lack a sideways twist.

Balsam Poplar *Populus balsamifera*

OTHER NAMES
Formerly known as *P. trichocarpa*. Also known as black poplar, black cottonwood, western balsam poplar, California poplar.

DESCRIPTION
GENERAL Deciduous tree.
SIZE Normally to 80' (24 m) high; trunk to 3' (90 cm) in diameter; occasionally to 197' (60 m) high; trunk to 6.6' (2 m) in diameter. See notes below.
LEAVES Simple, alternate, deciduous; shiny, dark green above, silvery below, ovate, pointed at tip, rounded to heart-shaped at base; leaf stalk round, to 6" (15 cm) long.
BARK Thin, smooth, grayish green when young, maturing to dark gray and thick, with deep longitudinal furrows.
FLOWERS Very small, in long, slender, loosely hanging catkins; sexes on separate trees appearing before leaves unfold; male catkins to 1.2" (3 cm) long, 20–30 stamens; female catkins to 4" (10 cm) long, 2 stigmas.
FRUIT Green capsules, egg-shaped, in hanging catkins; to 0.3" (8 mm) long; splits into 2–3 parts when ripe; seeds very small with a tuft of cottony hairs, dispersed in large masses by

KEY FEATURES
Leaves ovate; buds sticky; bark dark, thick, furrowed on mature trees.

Range.

the wind.

HABITAT
River valleys, stream banks, flood plains and similar low-lying sites.

RANGE
Alaska and Atlantic coast south to California and Virginia.

NOTES
The balsam poplar is the tallest native western hardwood. Cooler autumn temperatures trigger the change in leaf color to a brilliant yellow. This poplar was once thought to be a separate species from the black cottonwood—a larger coastal form. The black cottonwood (now identified as *Populus balsamifera trichocarpa*) is now regarded as the western subspecies of the balsam poplar.

Flower.

The largest specimen of the balsam poplar is currently found in Yamhill County, Oregon. It measures an amazing 147' (44.8 m) in height, and 30.2' (9.2 m) in trunk circumference.

Leaf.

Bark.

Trembling Aspen *Populus tremuloides*

OTHER NAMES
Also known as aspen, quaking aspen, white poplar, golden aspen, mountain aspen, popple, poplar and trembling poplar.

DESCRIPTION
GENERAL Deciduous tree.
SIZE Normally to 60' (18 m) high; trunk to 16" (40 cm) in diameter; occasionally to 100' (30 m) high; trunk to 24" (60 cm) in diameter.
LEAVES Simple, alternate, deciduous; fresh green above, paler beneath; round to heart-shaped, abruptly tipped, finely round-toothed, stalks long, slender, flattened; to 3" (7.5 cm) long.
BARK Thin, smooth, greenish white when young, maturing to gray or blackish, with dark longitudinal furrows on lower trunk. A powdery substance can be rubbed off young bark and used for protection from ultraviolet radiation.
FLOWERS Male and female on separate trees, appearing before leaves; catkins to 4" (10 cm) long. Male flowers with 6–12 stamens, bracts fringed with long hairs. Female flowers with 2 stigmas, bracts fringed with long hairs.

KEY FEATURES
Bark does not peel easily. Small round leaves on long stalks tremble in a breeze.

Range.

Flower.

FRUIT Cone-shaped capsules; capsule to 0.3" (7 mm) long; catkins to 4" (10 cm) long; many very small cotton-tipped seeds in each capsule.

HABITAT

Dry to moist sites, often in pure stands; low elevations to subalpine.

NOTES

Trembling aspen has amazing abilities of reproduction. Female trees can easily produce millions of seeds each year. The tiny seeds are carried by the wind for distances up to 20 miles (30 km) during a storm. Most trembling aspens, however, reproduce by suckering—a process in which the shallow roots produce new shoots. In the Pacific Northwest, cloning is the most common method of reproduction for this species. In fact the trembling aspen is considered by some to be one of the largest organisms in the world since it produces genetically identical clones that cover huge areas. This phenomenon can be easily viewed in spring or autumn, when all trees in a single clone leaf out or drop their leaves simultaneously.

The Aboriginal name for this species translates as "woman's tongue" or "noisy leaf."

Leaf.

Bark.

Plains Cottonwood *Populus deltoides monilifera*

OTHER NAMES
Formerly *P. deltoides occidentalis, P. sargentii.*

DESCRIPTION
GENERAL Deciduous tree.
SIZE Normally to 75' (22.5 m) high; trunk to 39" (1 m) in diameter; occasionally to 100' (30 m) high; trunk to 4' (1.2 m) in diameter.
LEAVES Simple, alternate, deciduous; bright shiny green above, paler beneath; broadly triangular, 20–25 rounded teeth per side, no teeth on tip or near stalk; stalk yellowish green, long and flattened; to 4" (10 cm) long.
BARK Thin, smooth, yellowish gray when young, maturing to dark gray, with deep longitudinal furrows.

FLOWERS Male and female flowers on separate trees into drooping catkins to 3" (7.5 cm) long, before leaves develop. Male (staminate) flowers occur in clusters of 2–4 catkins near tips of branches, bright red or yellow, cylindrical, with 20–60 reddish or yellowish stamens; female (pistillate) flowers produce individual catkins; green, cylindrical in shape, with a single ovoid pistil.

FRUIT Oval; each to 0.5" (1.2 cm) long, catkins to 10" (25 cm) long; splits into 3 or 4 parts when mature.

HABITAT
Rich, moist sites such as streambanks, or mixed with other species in open stands with species having similar requirements; low-lying sites.

RANGE
Southern British Columbia to Manitoba, south to Texas; low elevations.

NOTES
Aboriginal peoples used the roots for making fire. Recently it has been introduced in areas outside its native range (southern British Columbia, for example), where it colonizes riverbanks. This species develops very quickly into a rather robust tree capable of withstanding the harsh conditions associated with dry areas.

KEY FEATURES
Leaf is triangular with coarse teeth on the outer edges.

Bark.

Garry Oak *Quercus garryana*

OTHER NAMES
Also known as Oregon white oak, white oak.

DESCRIPTION
GENERAL Deciduous tree.
SIZE Normally to 66' (20 m) high; trunk to 35" (90 cm) in diameter; occasionally to 82' (25 m) high; trunk to 50" (1.5 cm) in diameter.
LEAVES Simple, alternate, deciduous; upper surface shiny dark green, greenish yellow and hairy below; 5–7 deeply round-lobed; to 6" (15 cm) long.
BARK Light gray with narrow furrows when young, maturing to dark gray with deeper furrows and stout scales.
FLOWERS Tiny yellow male and female flowers on the same tree; male flowers in hanging catkins, female flowers single or clustered; appear as the leaves sprout.
FRUIT Acorns; to 1.2" (3 cm) long; drop in the fall; edible.

HABITAT
Prefers dry, rocky south-facing slopes or bluffs, sometimes on rich soils; low elevations.

RANGE
Southern British Columbia south to southern California.

NOTES
The acorns of this oak were eaten by several Native peoples, often in the form of a meal or mush. The bitter tannins were removed by soaking the acorns in water. It was also used as one of the ingredients of a medicine used to treat tuberculosis and other ailments. Band-tailed pigeons, Steller's jays and other birds feed on the acorns. Several mammals, including Columbian black-tailed deer and deer mice, also feed on the acorns. Interestingly, the mountain lion has also been found to have acorns in the stomach, but it is unclear whether these instances were unusual.

KEY FEATURES
Leaves with 5–7 rounded lobes, acorns.

Bark.

81

Pacific Madrone *Arbutus menziesii*

OTHER NAMES
Also known as arbutus, madrone.

DESCRIPTION
GENERAL Broadleaf tree.

SIZE Normally to 66' (20 m) high; trunk to 16" (40 cm) in diameter; occasionally to 100' (30 m) high; trunk to 24" (60 cm) in diameter.

LEAVES Simple, alternate, evergreen; shiny dark green above, whitish green below, leathery; to 6" (15 cm) long.

BARK Thin, smooth and green when young, maturing to a distinctive reddish orange, peeling, freshly exposed surfaces yellowish green, turning to reddish orange; lower trunk of older specimens thicker and broken into many small flakes.

FLOWERS White, urn-shaped, fragrant (similar to buckwheat honey), to 0.3" (7 mm) long; in drooping clusters; appear with new leaves.

FRUIT Berry-like, orange-red, granular surface, many-seeded, in clusters, to 0.4" (1 cm) across.

HABITAT
Dry, sunny, rocky sites; intolerant of shade; low to middle elevations.

RANGE
Southern British Columbia south to Baja California.

NOTES
A sun-loving species that loses its bark rather than its leaves as the seasons progress. Also the only native broadleaf evergreen tree found in the Pacific Northwest. The second-year leaves turn reddish orange and begin falling shortly after the new crop of leaves is fully grown. As a result, the tree is always covered with leaves. The berry-like fruit is an important food for several birds including the dark-eyed junco, fox sparrow, varied thrush, band-tailed pigeon, quail and yellow-breasted chat. The fruit is also an important food for deer and other small mammals.

KEY FEATURES
Leaves evergreen, leather-like; bark thin, smooth, blotched, reddish orange, peeling.

Bark.

Oregon Ash *Fraxinus latifolia*

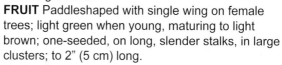

DESCRIPTION
GENERAL Deciduous tree.
SIZE Normally to 49' (15 m) high; trunk to 24" (60 cm) in diameter; occasionally to 82' (25 m) high; trunk to 3.3' (1 m) in diameter.
LEAVES Pinnately compound with 5–7 leaflets, opposite, deciduous; light green above, normally woolly beneath; leaflets to 6" (15 cm) long.
BARK Grayish with blotches when young, with welts; maturing with furrows and horizontal cracks.
FLOWERS Male and female flowers on separate trees; tiny to 0.1" (3 mm) across, in clusters, male flowers yellowish, female flowers greenish.
FRUIT Paddleshaped with single wing on female trees; light green when young, maturing to light brown; one-seeded, on long, slender stalks, in large clusters; to 2" (5 cm) long.
HABITAT
Prefers wet areas along streams and in canyons; low elevations.
RANGE
Northern Washington south to southern California; also present on Vancouver Island, British Columbia.

NOTES
An old superstition arose from the fact that poisonous snakes are unknown where this ash grows. Rattlesnakes were believed not to crawl over a branch or stick from this tree. Oregon ash has been known to reach the age of 250 years—only growing quickly during the first third of its life. The seeds are eaten by grouse, ducks, finches and other birds. Ash wood is used for making flooring, millwork, crates, baseball bats, tool handles and other items.

> **KEY FEATURES**
> Fruit is paddle-shaped with a single wing.

Bark.

Pin Cherry *Prunus pensylvanica*

DESCRIPTION
GENERAL Deciduous tree or tall shrub.
SIZE Normally to 16' (5 m) high; trunk to 6" (15 cm) in diameter; occasionally to 50' (15 m) high; trunk to 12" (30 cm) in diameter.
LEAVES Simple, alternate, deciduous; shiny yellowish green; lance-shaped with long, gradual taper to slender sharp tip; minute, uneven teeth; to 4" (10 cm) long; often turning bright red in fall.
BARK Shiny, dark reddish brown when young; maturing to shed horizontal papery strips; horizontal markings (lenticels).
FLOWERS White; saucer-shaped with 5 petals; to 0.5" (1.4 cm) across; clusters of 5–7 on stalks.
FRUIT Bright red; to 0.3" (8 mm) across; small hanging clusters.

HABITAT
Sun-loving species; in areas recently cleared by cutting or burning, and along rivers; found as individual trees.

RANGE
Southern Northwest Territories to Colorado.

NOTES
As with all cherries (*Prunus*), all parts of this tree, except the fruit, contain hydrocyanic acid, which can cause cyanide poisoning. Do not eat the stones. This poison is so strong that crushed leaves or strips of bark will kill insects in an enclosed space.

Fruit & leaves.

Pin cherries are often collected in large quantities and made into jelly or wine. The fruit can be eaten raw, but it is quite tart. A gum-like substance exuded by the trunk was once used as a chewing gum.

> **KEY FEATURES**
> Large, slender leaves with long, tapering points.

Bark of young tree.

Bitter Cherry *Prunus emarginata*

OTHER NAME
Also known as bittercherry.

DESCRIPTION
GENERAL Deciduous tree.
SIZE Normally to 49' (15 m) high; trunk to 8" (20 cm) in diameter; occasionally to 66' (20 m) high; trunk to 28" (70 cm) in diameter.
LEAVES Simple, alternate, deciduous; yellowish green; oblong to oval; fine, rounded teeth; to 3" (8 cm) long; 2 small knobs (glands) at base of stem.
BARK Thin, smooth, shiny, reddish brown with prominent raised lenticels in horizontal rows when young, maturing to grayish brown, lightly roughened and marked with grayish lenticels.

FLOWERS
White or pinkish; form clusters of 5–12; clusters to 6" (15 cm) across; flowers appear when leaves are half-grown.

FRUIT
Bright red cherries; bitter tasting; to 0.5" (1 cm) across; each fruit on a short stem in clusters from a long central stem.

HABITAT
On poor soils near streams, on logged areas and in moist montane forests; at low to middle elevations.

RANGE
Central British Columbia to northern California, west to Montana.

NOTES
Bitter cherry bark was peeled off in narrow strips and used in ornamental basketwork by Aboriginal peoples. The fruit of this species matures in July or August but the cherries are so bitter they are inedible. This tree is an excellent addition to the backyard since the fruit attracts a wide variety of birds, including grouse, band-tailed pigeons, flickers, jays, robins, waxwings, tanagers, orioles and mourning doves.

KEY FEATURES
Small, oval leaves without points; flat-topped clusters of white flowers; bright red berries.

SIMILAR SPECIES
Choke Cherry *Prunus virginiana* is a deciduous shrub that reaches 13' (4 m) tall with white, bottle brush-like flowers in clusters to 6" (15 cm) long; shiny, dark, round berry-like drupes are produced in clusters.

Black Hawthorn *Crataegus douglasii*

OTHER NAMES

Also known as Douglas hawthorn, river hawthorn, western thorn apple, and Douglas thorntree.

DESCRIPTION

GENERAL Thorny deciduous tree or tall shrub; may have multiple stems from the base or a single stem that branches just above ground. Thorns short, normally less than 1.25 " (3 cm) long.

SIZE Normally to 20' (6 m) high; trunk to 6" (15 cm) in diameter; occasionally to 36' (11 m) high; trunk to 12" (30 cm) in diameter.

LEAVES Simple, alternate, deciduous; shiny dark green; lanceolate to obovate, serrate to doubly serrate; to 3.75" (9.5 cm) long.

BARK Thin, rough, gray to brown when young; matures to very rough with scaly appearance. Resembles Pacific crabapple.

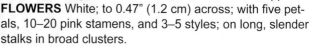

FLOWERS White; to 0.47" (1.2 cm) across; with five petals, 10–20 pink stamens, and 3–5 styles; on long, slender stalks in broad clusters.

FRUIT Apple-like, dark reddish purple to black pomes; to 0.47" (1.2 cm) across; light yellow pulp with 3–5 nutlets.

HABITAT

Thrives in a variety of areas with moist soil conditions.

RANGE

Southern Alaska to northern California.

NOTES

Flowers of black hawthorn sometimes emit a somewhat fishy odor. Native peoples used the small thorns for lancing boils, piercing ears and producing fish hooks. They also prepared a poultice with chewed leaves to relieve swelling, and made other remedies for stomach problems.

KEY FEATURES
A small tree with small, sharp spines; zig-zag twigs.

SIMILAR SPECIES

Fireberry Hawthorn *Crataegus chrysocarpa*, a tall shrub with reddish (occasionally yellowish) fruit and long, slender thorns that reach 2.4" (6 cm) in length. This species may be encountered from Oregon south to New Mexico, north to Alberta to the East Coast.

Pacific Crab Apple *Malus fusca*

OTHER NAMES
Formerly *Pyrus fusca, M. diversifolia*; also known as Pacific crabapple, wild crab apple, Oregon crab apple.

DESCRIPTION
GENERAL Deciduous tree or tall shrub.
SIZE Normally to 30' (9 m) high; trunk to 12" (30 cm) in diameter; occasionally to 39' (12 m) high; trunk to 14" (36 cm) in diameter; often with several trunks.
LEAVES Simple, alternate, deciduous; shiny green; lance to egg-shaped; sharply toothed; to 4" (10 cm) long; turns red or orange in fall.
BARK Thin, reddish brown and scaly when young, maturing to brown with deep fissures.
FLOWERS 5 rounded white or pink petals; to 1" (2.5 cm) across; 5–12 in flat-topped clusters on spur-shoots; showy and fragrant.
FRUIT Oblong pomes (small apples) are present in clusters; each to 0.75" (1.9 cm) long; greenish at first, later turning yellowish or reddish; edible but tart.

HABITAT
Moist woods, swamps, water edges, upper beaches, estuary fringes and in coniferous forests; low to middle elevations.

RANGE
Southern Alaska to central California.

NOTES
The Pacific crab apple was an important food for most coastal peoples. Apples were eaten fresh or stored under water, or under a mixture of water and oil, in storage boxes made from cedar. The acidity of this fruit keeps them remarkably well using this technique. In fact, they become softer and sweeter over time. Native peoples used the bark for a wide variety of medicinal treatments for the eyes and for stomach and digestive ailments. The bark and seeds contain cyanide-producing compounds and should only be used with extreme caution. The fruit, however, does not contain any cyanide-producing compounds.
Caution: Seeds contain cyanide and are poisonous if eaten. The fruit is also sought after by several bird species.

KEY FEATURES
Found in or near wetlands; distinctive fragrant flowers or clusters of very small apples.

Bark.

Pacific Dogwood *Cornus nuttallii*

OTHER NAMES
Also known as flowering dogwood, western flowering dogwood, mountain dogwood, mountain flowering dogwood.

DESCRIPTION
GENERAL Deciduous tree.
SIZE Normally to 30' (9 m) high; trunk to 12" (30 cm) in diameter; occasionally to 66' (20 m) high; trunk to 24" (61 cm) in diameter.
LEAVES Simple, opposite, deciduous; deep green; oval, sharp-pointed, to 6" (15 cm) long, veins curve parallel to leaf edge.
BARK Thin, smooth, light gray to reddish brown when young, maturing with ridges and small plates.
FLOWERS Tiny, dull purple or green, in clusters surrounded by 4–6 large, white showy floral bracts; to 8" (20 cm) across; flowers in the spring, and often again in early fall.

FRUIT Central flowers develop into a compact cluster of 30–40 bright red drupes (berries); each to 0.4" (1 cm) long.

HABITAT
Well-drained sites, often along streams and riverbanks in open to fairly dense stands, usually mixed forest.

RANGE
Southern British Columbia to southern California.

NOTES
The fruit of the Pacific dogwood is favored by band-tailed pigeons, quail, grosbeaks, hermit thrush, flickers and waxwings, so it is an excellent addition to backyards. It also has large, striking flowers. Native people prepared the bark of this species to purify the blood, strengthen the lungs and treat stomach troubles. In the past, Native peoples used the wood for making bows and arrows, and the bark as a tanning agent. The blossom of is species is the floral emblem of British Columbia.

Flowers.

Bark.

> **KEY FEATURES**
> Leaves with veins curving parallel to leaf edge, large white flowers and clusters of red "berries."

Cascara *Rhamnus purshiana*

OTHER NAMES
Formerly *R. purshianus, Frangula purshiana*; Also known as Cascara buckthorn.
DESCRIPTION
GENERAL Deciduous tree or tall shrub.
SIZE Normally to 20' (6 m) high; trunk to 10" (25 cm) in diameter; occasionally to 33' (10 m) high; trunk to 12" (30 cm) in diameter.
LEAVES Simple, alternate, deciduous; green above, pale green below; oval, parallel veins curving forward; tip short, base rounded; to 6.3" (16 cm) long.
BARK Thin, smooth, mottled gray bark when young, maturing to become scaly.
FLOWERS Yellowish green, small.
FRUIT Berry-like drupes; blackish, to 0.6" (14 mm) across.
HABITAT
Mainly on moist sites, burned areas, clearings and in conifer forests, where it is an understory species.

RANGE
Southern British Columbia to northern California; east to northern Idaho and NW Montana.
NOTES
Cascara bark was once harvested for the drug cascara sagrada, a natural

Fruit.

laxative that was highly regarded for many decades. The bark of this tree was also used by Native peoples as a laxative, and as a treatment for a wide range of other ailments. The ruffed grouse, band-tailed pigeon and other birds feed on the drupes, and one study from British Columbia found that coastal deer readily feed on this fruit while most other ungulates (members of the deer family) do not.

KEY FEATURES
Leaves oval with veins curving forward, fruits berry-like, blackish.

Bark.

Glossary

bract (cone): modified leaf at the base of a cone. In some conifers, such as firs (*Abies*), bracts are interspersed among cone scales.

glabrous: without hairs, hairless, smooth.

inflorescence: cluster of flowers arranged on a single stem.

layering: process in which a lower branch produces new roots that grow into the ground.

pedicle: stalk of a single flower.

peduncle: stalk or stem of a single flower or inflorescence.

pendulous: hanging downward.

petiole: stalk or stem of a leaf; leafstalk.

pistillate: describes a female flower: having one or more pistils but with out functional stamens.

pollen cones: male cones that contain pollen; normally shorter lived than seed cones.

pubescent: with hairs attached, hairy.

raceme: hanging cylindrical cluster of flowers.

scale: small, thin or flat structure.

seed cone: female or ovulate cone, usually larger and lasting longer than pollen cones.

sessile: describes flowers or leaves: without a stalk.

staminate: male flower.

stomata: tiny pores used for gas exchange.

Acknowledgements & Credits

I would like to thank several people who assisted with this project.

Mary Schendlinger for her careful editing.
Jim Salt, who generously aided me in locating several tree species for photography.
Steven MacRae at Lethbridge College who provided valuable input for limber pine.
The skilled photographers who provided photos. Their names appear below.
        Cliff Wallis 84 t,m
        Thomas Palmer 84 b
        Susan Servos-Sept 95

Bibliography

Brayshaw, Christopher. 1996. *Trees and Shrubs of British Columbia.* Royal BC Museum, Victoria BC.

Farrar, John Laird. 1995. *Trees in Canada.* Fitzhenry and Whiteside Ltd. and Canadian Forest Service, Natural Resources, Canada.

Hosie, R.C. 1990. *Native Trees of Canada.* Fitzhenry & Whiteside in cooperation with the Canadian Forest Service.

Johnson, Derek, Linda Kershaw, Andy MacKinnon and Jim Pojar. 1995. *Plants of the Western Boreal Forest and Aspen Parkland.* Lone Pine Publishing, Edmonton AB.

Kershaw, L., Andy MacKinnon and Jim Pojar. 1998. *Plants of the Rocky Mountains.* Lone Pine Publishing, Edmonton AB.

Lyons, C.P., and Bill Merrilees. 1995. *Trees, Shrubs, & Flowers to Know in Washington & British Columbia.* Lone Pine Publishing, Edmonton AB.

Parish, R., R. Coupe and D. Lloyd. 1996. *Plants of the Southern Interior of BC.* BC Ministry of Forests and Lone Pine Publishing, Edmonton AB.

Pojar, Jim, and Andy MacKinnon. 1994. *Plants of the Pacific Northwest Coast: Washington, Oregon, British Columbia, and Alaska.* Lone Pine Publishing, Edmonton AB.

Index

About the Author

Duane Sept is a biologist, freelance writer and professional photographer. His biological work has included research on various wildlife species and service as a park naturalist. His award-winning photographs have been published internationally, in displays and in books, magazines and other publications, for clients that include BBC Wildlife, Parks Canada, Nature Canada, National Wildlife Federation and World Wildlife Fund.

Today Duane brings a wealth of information to the public as an author, in much the same way he has inspired thousands of visitors to Canada's parks. His published books include The Beachcomber's Guide to Seashore Life in the Pacific Northwest (Harbour Publishing), Wild Berries of the Northwest: Alaska, Western Canada and the Northwestern United States (Calypso Publishing) and Common Mushrooms of the Northwest: Alaska, Western Canada and the Northwestern United States (Calypso Publishing).

More Great Books from Calypso Publishing

Wild Berries of the Northwest:
Alaska, Western Canada and the Northwestern United States

J. Duane Sept

Fruits and berries are all around us. Identify these fruits and their flowers on your next trip to the ocean, lake or woods with this full-color guide. Learn which species are edible and which are poisonous. An entire chapter of mouth-watering recipes is also featured. Enjoy!

5.5" x 8.5" • 96 pages • 169 color photos • Softcover • $14.95 • ISBN 978-0-9739819-3-3

••••••••••••••••••••••••

Common Mushrooms of the Northwest:
Alaska, Western Canada and the Northwestern United States

J. Duane Sept

This full-color photographic guide features 130 species of mushrooms and other fungi found in the Northwest, from Alaska to Oregon—some edible, some poisonous, all intriguing. Besides a description of each species, the book includes habitat, range, edibility, tips on distinguishing similar species and other interesting information. There are also pointers on storing edible mushrooms, making spore prints and much more.

5.5" x 8.5" • 96 pages • 150 color photos • Softcover • $14.95 • ISBN 978-0-9739819-0-2

••••••••••••••••••••••••

Common Wildflowers of the Pacific Northwest:
British Columbia, Washington and Oregon

J. Duane Sept

The glorious wildflowers of the Pacific Northwest are as diverse and interesting as their habitats. Who would guess that one species blooms every spring, and another may take as many as 17 summers to produce a single flower? Information and fascinating facts on each flower are included, and a full-color wildflower photo guide aids in matching flowers to photos. The Pacific Northwest is rich with wildflowers, and with this clear, beautiful new guide, identification for 231 species has never been easier!

5.5" x 8.5" • 96 pages • 250+ color photos • Softcover • $14.95 • ISBN 978-0-9952266-1-6

These titles are available at your local bookstore or

Calypso Publishing

www.calypso-publishing.com